LET'S GO MEET MY MOM

SHE'S U[...]
I'LL BE [...]
30 YE[...]

YOU MEET ALL MY FRIENDS.

& THEY LIKE YOU. JUST ENOUGH

WE COULD GET IT ON

O[...]

INEVITABLE.

HAVE SOME KIDS

WE GO BACK HOME TO OUR PARTNERS

& HAVE NICE LIVES.

WHO DIED YOUNG

I COULD MAKE YOU DINNER

THIS IS REAL

& NAME THEM AFTER ROCK STARS

CONTROL OURSELVES... & CONTINUE GROCERY SHOPPING

YOU COULD TELL ME ALL ABOUT YOUR [P]ET GOLDFISH

WE WATCH YOUR FAVORITE MOVIE & I PRETEND I GET IT.

I HURT YOU.

& YOUR DREAMS OF TRAVELING TO MARS...

REAL BAD.

[T]ALK [E]VERY [D]AY

YOU CAN STOP WONDERING WHO YOU WILL GROW OLD WITH...

YOU COULD BE CRAZY.

ME. DUH.

WE JUST STAY HERE.

BUT THATS MY TYPE.

I TELL YOU MY DREAMS & YOU LISTEN LIKE IT'S INTERESTING

all OF MY
HEART, I MEAN
EVERY LAST BIT
BELONGS IN THE
ARMS OF:

I LIKE you,
I LOVE you.

by
carissa
potter

CHRONICLE BOOKS
SAN FRANCISCO

Library of Congress Cataloging-in-Publication Data:
Names: Potter, Carissa, author, artist.
Title: I like you/I love you / By Carissa Potter.
Description: San Francisco : Chronicle Books, 2016.
Identifiers: LCCN 2015040353 | ISBN 9781452144986
Subjects: LCSH: Love-letters. | Interpersonal relations. | Artists' books—
California—Oakland.
Classification: LCC N7433.4.P68 | 2016 | DDC 700.9794/66—dc23 LC
record available at http://lccn.loc.gov/2015040353

Manufactured in China

10 9 8 7 6 5 4 3 2 1

Chronicle books and gifts are available at special quantity discounts to
corporations, professional associations, literacy programs, and other
organizations. For details and discount information, please contact our
premiums department at corporatesales@chroniclebooks.com or at
1-800-759-0190.

Chronicle Books LLC
680 Second Street
San Francisco, CA 94107

www.chroniclebooks.com

IN ALL SERIOUSNESS

AS YOU READ THIS,
I ENCOURAGE YOU TO
EXPLORE THE SUBTLE
TRANSITIONS OF
RELATIONSHIPS FROM
INITIAL ATTRACTION
THROUGH COMPROMISES,
ALL THE WAY TO CHOOSING
TO GROW TOGETHER.

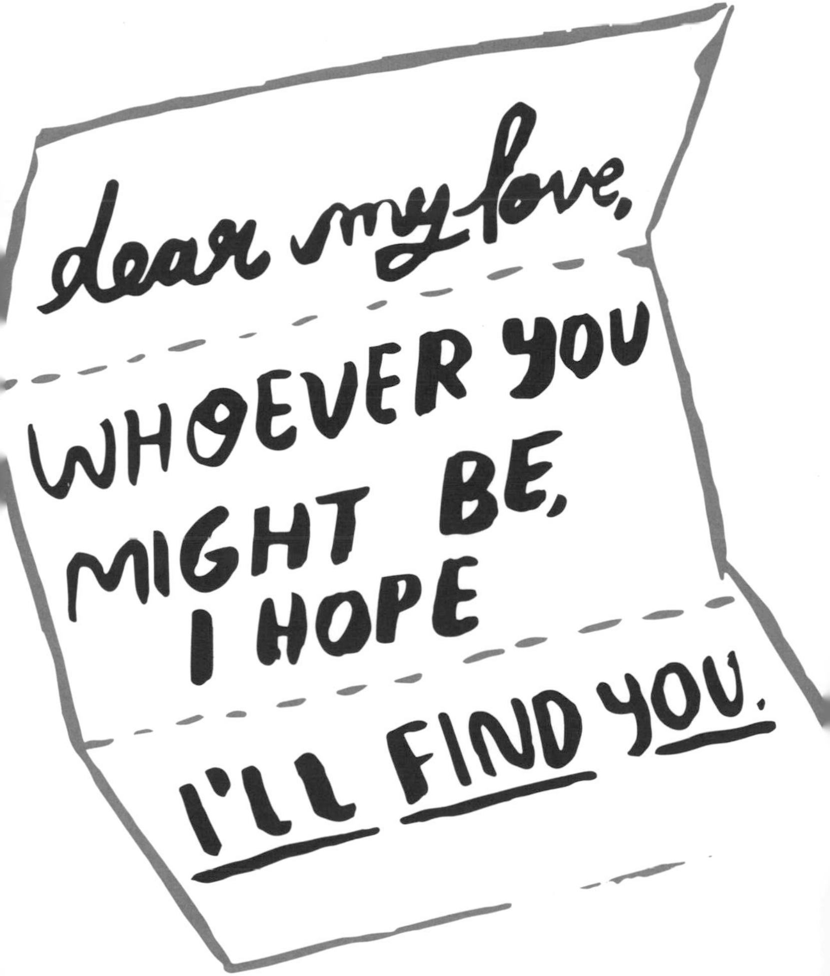
dear my love,
WHOEVER YOU
MIGHT BE,
I HOPE
I'LL FIND YOU.

FEAR OF MISSING OUT

(ON YOU)

BASIC RELATIONSHIP ALCHEMY

IN ANOTHER LIFE, WE
MAY NEVER HAVE MET,
LUCKY FOR US, IN THIS
ONE WE DID.

THE ODDS ARE
IN YOUR FAVOR.
(Studies show that
people like people who like
them back)

YOU <u>DON'T</u> HAVE
TO BRING FLOWERS,
YOU JUST HAVE TO
SHOW UP...

TO CALL, OR
NOT TO CALL,
OR WAIT TO CALL,
OR TEXT? OR
FACEBOOK MESSAGE,
GCHAT,
EMAIL,
TWEET,
POST, AFTER
THE FIRST
DATE???

LONELY
ME

REMNANTS
FROM THE PAST
(last night's dinner)

YOU
ATE IT
ALL...

& said "IT WAS THE BEST DARN SPAGHETTI" EVEN THOUGH I WAS TRYING TO MAKE LASAGNA.

OUR CONNECTION IS REAL.

HOW JOKES WORK

"WHAT KIND OF BEES
MAKE MILK NOT
HONEY?"

"DUNNO."

"BOOBIES!"*

*SAID BY YOU, THIS IS SO AMAZING & FUNNY

*SAID BY ANYONE ELSE, IT'S STUPID & POSSIBLY BORDERLINE OFFENSIVE.

YOUR
HANDS

MY
HEART

MY IDEAL SCHEDULE

Z z z Z Z

actually

I ^actually ENJOYED
NOT BEING
ABLE TO SLEEP
'CUZ YOU SNORE.*

I KNOW YOU THINK I LOOK NICE WHEN YOU HOLD MY HAND ON THE STREET, EVEN THOUGH YOU NEVER SAID IT OUT LOUD...

YOU'RE NOT MY
DREAM PERSON.

YOU'RE MY DREAMS
COME TRUE PERSON.

HOW EXACTLY DO YOU KNOW WHEN IT'S <u>LOVE</u>?

OUR 1st SILENCE

looked like nothing...

...but felt
like everything.

↖ THE UNIVERSE

WE MOVED
IN WITH
EACH OTHER...

MOVING IN WITH SOMEONE

IS KINDA LIKE MAKING A PACT THAT YOU ARE BOTH GOING TO MAKE AN EFFORT TO KEEP YOUR LOVE & HOUSEPLANTS ALIVE.

"OUR"
MISC.
SPORTS
DECOR

JORD-
AN

23

or who-
ever

"OUR" FLOWER PATTERN FINE CHINA COLLECTION

THE TABLE WE PICKED OUT TOGETHER

THE 1st I TOLD YOU I LOVED YOU THERE WAS ALWAYS THE CHANCE IT WAS A MISTAKE, THE 2nd TIME I TOLD YOU I KNEW THERE WAS NO GOING BACK...

CLOSENESS:

COMMITMENT:
YOU SAVE
SUNDAYS FOR ME

I TELL YOU
EVERYTHING
EVEN WHEN
I SHOULDN'T

CRAVING:
I CAN'T
GET ENOUGH
OF YOU

OH THE HORROR!

NOW YOU HAVE SOMEONE TO BRING YOU COFFEE IN BED! (THEORETICALLY)

I WOULDN'T CHANGE A THING ABOUT YOU

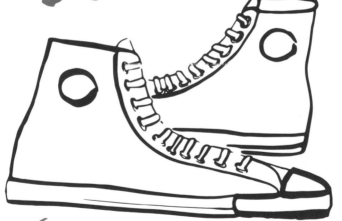

(BUT YOU COULD GET RID OF A FEW PAIRS OF SHOES...)

HONEY, WHY DID YOU LEAVE THOSE COOKIE CRUMBS ON THE PLATE?

BASICALLY CLEAN

OH, I WAS JUST SAVING THEM FOR YOU.

PROBLEM OF SPENDING TOO MUCH TIME WITH 1 PERSON

"YOU HAVE TO CHANGE."
"BUT I GOT DRESSED FIRST."

ALONE TIME

SOMETIMES YOU
NEED IT & IT'S
OKAY

I DON'T NEED YOU

BUT
I
WANT
YOU.

PERFECT
SPLIT

YOU SAY ALL
PEOPLE SHOULD LIKE
BATON & YET I DON'T...

FRUIT 4 ME, EGGS ARE WEIRD

BACON &
EGGS
4 YOU

the SLOW DANCE

on a crowded floor,
there is just our rhythm...

all this time only
makes it stronger

A STORY
OF
A
HAPPY
RELATIONSHIP

INCLUDES:
1. HAVING NEW
EXCITING EXPERIENCES
TOGETHER.
2. TOUCH. HOLDING.
SEX. EVEN SCHEDULED.
3. FOCUSING ON
THE GOOD THINGS
ABOUT EACH OTHER.

WE'RE

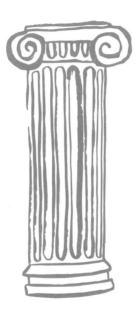

CLASSIC

I CAN TAKE
ON ANYTHING,
KNOWING
YOU BELIEVE
IN ME...

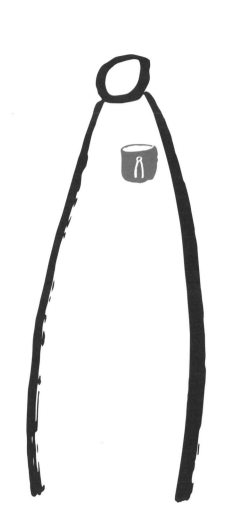

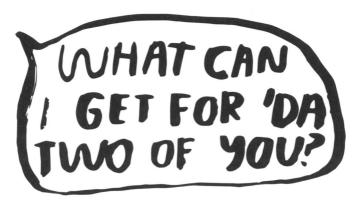

THE THINGS YOU
DO FOR LOVE.

my
SIDE

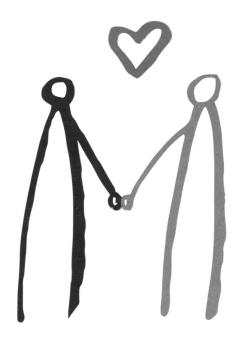

~~YOUR~~ SIDE
OUR

FADE
INTO

EACH
OTHER

IT'S
YOU
I WANNA SEE.

FOR THE FIRST
TIME IN KNOWN
HISTORY PEOPLE ARE
GETTING TOGETHER
NOT FOR MONEY,
FAMILY, OR LAW.

PEOPLE ARE
TOGETHER FOR
LOVE AND TO
BE HAPPY.

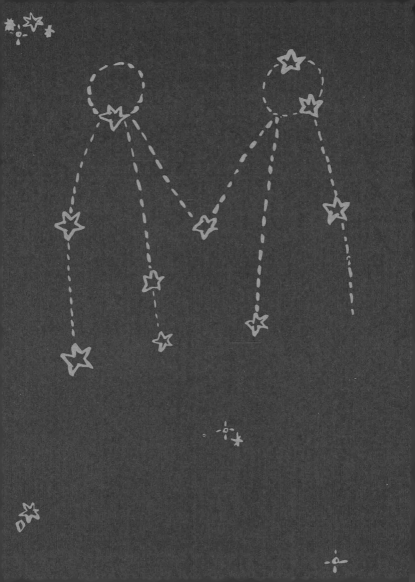

WE WERE
MEANT
TO BE

<u>ON A</u>
<u>PERSONAL</u>
<u>NOTE</u>

THIS BOOK IS FOR JOSH.

HIS FAVORITE CONVERSATION:

ME: "HOW DID YOU KNOW YOU LIKED ME?"

JOSH: "I DON'T KNOW."

ME: "BUT HOW DID YOU FEEL???"

JOSH: "I DON'T KNOW."

ME: "LIKE WERE YOU HAPPY TO SEE ME?"

JOSH: "I DON'T KNOW."

ME: "HOW DID YOU KNOW YOU LOVED ME? HUH? HUH?"

JOSH: "I JUST DON'T KNOW, CARISSA."

I FORGET HOW I KNOW THAT THIS IS LOVE?

I TELL MYSELF NOT TO BRING THAT UP AGAIN.

WHILE I ING DE INTO M EYES

UNTIL YOU SAY IT

HOPE IN M DIRE

AND NOT LIKE.

I TELL YOU I LOVE YOU. AGAINST MY BETTER JUDGEMENT.

I GUESS I CAN'T GO ON THAT HOT DATE NEXT WEEK

WE C BAC EATI PIZZ

JUST COULDN'T HOLD IT INSIDE ME

WITH THAT HOTTIE

& YOU SAY "THANKS."

OH, YEAH, I FORGOT YOU ARE MY HOTTIE

WE WORK AT OUR LOVE.

LIKE A JOB.

EVERYDAY I MAKE IT A PRIORITY.

WE COULD BOTH WALK IN DIFFERENT DIRECTIONS

ONE THAT I WAS MEANT TO DO.

UNTIL WE MEET UP AGAIN

OR MAYBE WE DON'T.

V H A T

WE COULD FREEZE OURSELVES, JUST LIKE THIS

& WE BOTH ARE HAPPY ALONE

O

FOR FUTURE GENERATIONS

WITH SOM NE

TO KNOW L